# TIME TRAVEL

## HOW TO BE THE BEST
## TIME TRAVELLER EVER

Buster Books

Written by Lottie Stride
Illustrated by Dusan Pavlic
Edited by Sally Pilkington and Imogen Williams
Designed by Barbara Ward
Cover design by John Bigwood
History Consultant Dr Kevin Meek
With thanks to Alanna Skuse

First published in Great Britain in 2018 by Buster Books,
an imprint of Michael O'Mara Books Limited,
9 Lion Yard, Tremadoc Road, London SW4 7NQ

 www.busterbooks.co.uk  Buster Children's Books ✔ @BusterBooks

A CIP catalogue record for this book is available from the British Library.

ISBN: 978–1–78055–507–2

1 3 5 7 9 10 8 6 4 2

This book was printed in March 2018 by 1010 Printing International Ltd, 1010 Avenue, Xia Nan Industrial District, Yuan Zhou Town, Bo Luo County, Hui Zhou City, Guang Dong Province, China.

## INTRODUCTION

This book contains all the skills you'll need to become the world's best time traveller. You'll learn everything from how to make papyrus in ancient Greece, to building a Viking longship and surviving the Black Death.

When you've read this book from start to finish, sign the certificate at the back of the book to show off your new know-how skills.

## SAFE TRAVELS

The hints and tips in this book are intended for practice purposes only. Under no circumstances should you ever attempt any exercise that would put yourself or others in any danger in real life.

We urge you, at all times, to make yourself aware of, and obey, all laws, regulations and local by-laws, and respect all rights, including the rights of property owners. Always respect other people's privacy and remember to ask a responsible adult for assistance and take their advice whenever necessary.

# CONTENTS

# WELCOME TO
# TIME TRAVEL

Welcome. Your very first journey
through time is about to begin.

Leap button

This is your time-travel (TT)
handset. It's an amazing and
essential piece of equipment for
all time travellers. In this book, you
are going to use its LEAP button,
which will catapult you back to
any point in time and to any place
in the world. When you arrive,
check the handset's screen to find
out what year you have landed in.

# TIME TRAVEL DOS AND DON'TS

To help you get the most out of your time travels, here are some dos and don'ts:

- **DO** take very good care of your TT handset. When not in use, keep it in a secure pocket or, even better, attach it to your belt. If you lose it, there is NO WAY BACK HOME. The handset is state-of-the-art technology, so it is pretty unlikely that you will be able to pick up a new one in ancient Egypt.

- **DON'T** worry if you feel a bit strange or dizzy upon landing the first few times. It's perfectly normal. Not everyone enjoys the sensation of whizzing through time straight away. Like most things, time travel gets easier each time you do it.

- **DO** treat any people you meet on your travels with respect. They may not have computers, or even metal tools, but that doesn't mean they're stupid – they're just living in an earlier time than you. Asking them if they like football or pop music, or even if you can borrow their mobile phone, will make you very unpopular, and they will probably think you are totally mad.

Unfortunately, the EJECT button will only send you back to the present day. It won't get you out of hot water if your parents have just discovered a mess in your bedroom. You will have to deal with that yourself.

Eject button

EJECT

Activating the EJECT button will shoot you out of harm's way, then fast-forward you back home.

- **DON'T** hesitate to hit the large red EJECT button in the centre of your handset any time you feel threatened or scared. Don't hang around – the past can be a dangerous place.

- **DO** speak normally. Your handset is equipped with a state-of-the-art programme called BlabberSpeak. BlabberSpeak automatically adjusts to the language of the time and place you land in. With BlabberSpeak enabled, you will be able to both understand and speak to the people you meet on your travels as long as you are holding the handset, or it is attached to your belt.

- **DON'T** panic. Your clothes will travel through time with you. You won't find yourself stark naked and chatting to Henry VIII.

- **DO** breathe freely. The TT handset is equipped with an ImmunoShield. This helps protect you from catching the bugs of the past, and also stops you giving modern coughs and colds to people you meet on your travels.

- **DO** consult this book before you go, and keep it with you during your visit. It will provide you with top tips and essential time-tourist information, highlighting must-see sights and things that are in your best interests to avoid.

## WARNING

Do not try to change the course of history, no matter how tempting it is. Time travel is not to be used for personal gain, other than for gaining knowledge.

Going back in time to buy a lottery ticket after finding out this week's numbers is strictly forbidden. Your TT belt will know about it and take immediate action by transporting you back to ancient Rome to roast rodents for supper (see pages 104 to 107). It will not return you home until it is convinced you have seen the error of your ways.

Now you're ready to go.

Take a deep breath and press the LEAP button.

### GOOD LUCK, AND ENJOY YOUR TRAVELS!

# HOW TO ...

## 1588 CE

# BEAT THE SPANISH ARMADA

The wind is blasting your ears, and you are swaying about like part of a circus act. You've landed in the 'crow's nest' of an English warship. Unfortunately a crow's nest is a little lookout platform three-quarters of the way up the ship's mast.

All around you are other ships racing through the waves. Your ship is part of an English fleet chasing the mighty warships of a fleet known as The Spanish Armada away from the English coast.

## TOP TACTICS

You're spotted, and the sailors suspect you of being a stowaway. They take you to the commander, Sir Charles Howard. Unfortunately, he has been known to 'keelhaul' rebellious sailors – having them dragged beneath the ship using a rope. This would cut them to ribbons on the barnacles below. Luckily, he's in a good mood. After months of fierce fighting, the Spanish are on the run. So he's quite happy to quaff a tot of rum and tell you his tactics:

- Sir Charles is using fast, nimble ships. The Spanish galleons are much bigger, and when it comes to twisting and turning, they are a lot slower.

- The English crews are experienced sailors, whereas the Spanish have packed their ships with soldiers. The Spanish plan is to get close to the enemy ships and board them, but the English sail their ships too well to let the Spanish get near.

- Sir Charles is making good use of cannons. The English go in really close, attack the Spanish from the sides, and fire at short range. They have better long-range guns, too, which means they can fire more accurately at the Spanish from further away.

- Sir Charles' commanders have had a brainwave. One night they set eight of the oldest ships alight. The wind blew them into the Spanish fleet and the Spanish were forced to sail off up the coast to get away from them.

# LIFE AFLOAT

Life on board seems so exciting, you decide to join the crew for supper. Unfortunately, first on the menu is salted meat and soggy biscuits with little bugs called weevils in them. As night falls, a crew of 40 men eating, fighting and sleeping in the same clothes for months on end does not make below deck smell good. After one night in the dark, damp, squashed, smelly ship you will never complain about sharing a room with your brother or sister again.

# WHAT 'KNOT' TO DO

In the morning, a sailor tells you Sir Charles has insisted you earn your keep. He shows you how to tie some essential knots, including a bowline, which is used to attach a rope to a post or railing.

1   Make a small loop a little way along the rope. It helps if you imagine the loop is a rabbit 'hole', the tip of the rope is the 'rabbit' itself, and the rest of the rope is a 'tree'.

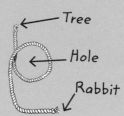

2   Feed the rabbit up through the hole as shown.

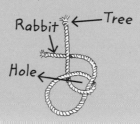

3   Pass the rabbit round the back of the tree.

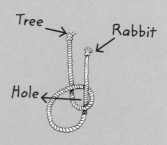

4   Pass the rabbit down into the hole.

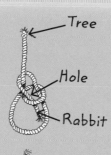

5   Pull it tight.

**700 BCE**

# MAKE SILK
# IN ANCIENT CHINA

Yuck! All around you are wooden trays packed with pale sandy-greyish maggoty worms. There are millions of them – munching on leaves and wriggling about in their own droppings.

You've landed in ancient China, right in the middle of a silkworm farm. Beside you, a girl is fishing a silkworm out of one of the trays. Her name is Mei Ying and she tells you that the worms are not actually worms at all, but caterpillars of the silk moth. The caterpillars are eating mulberry leaves, and have been eating non-stop for about six weeks. They hatched from tiny little eggs and have shed their skin four times to become the fat caterpillars they are now.

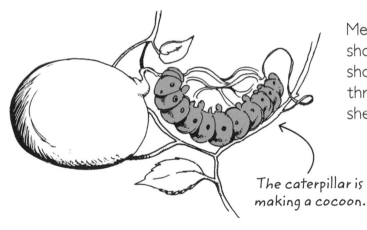

Mei Ying picks one up to show it to you up close. It is shooting what looks like little threads out of its mouth, and she tells you that this is silk.

The caterpillar is making a cocoon.

Mei Ying puts the caterpillar into a wooden frame next to lots of others that have already finished their cocoons. She says that the silk is actually the caterpillar's hardened saliva or spit. Each caterpillar wraps itself in up to a kilometre of silk. She holds up a finished cocoon, and explains the caterpillar inside is busy turning itself into a moth. Unfortunately, none of these caterpillars will ever be a moth.

She leads you to a large pan of boiling water, which contains lots of the finished cocoons bobbing about like white cotton wool balls. The cocoons are thrown in there while they are still alive, killing the caterpillar inside and making the thread easier to work with. Mei Ying says the cocoons are ready for her mum to work on. She gets some chopsticks and starts fishing cocoons out of the pan and putting them in a basket. This looks very easy, but when you have a go you keep dropping them back in.

Mei Ying hears a noise and asks you to hide – she will be in great danger if she is found talking to you. The process of spinning the caterpillar cocoons into silk thread and weaving it into cloth is a closely guarded secret. The Chinese are the only people in the world who know how to do it, and they make lots of money from trading their fine cloth all over the world. Revealing the secret is punishable by death. From your hiding place, you see Mei Ying's mother come in.

She takes a cocoon from the basket, and sits at a kind of spinning wheel. She examines the cocoon, looking for the end of the silk thread. When she finds it, she uses a silk reel to unravel the cocoon.

As you watch, you find it hard to believe that little fat caterpillars can produce so much thread. Mei Ying tells you that even though a single caterpillar can produce nearly a whole kilometre of thread, it is so fine that it can take up to 100 of them to make a single scarf.

Next Mei Ying's mother twists five or six silk threads together to form a stronger thread. These can then be dyed different colours and used for embroidery or woven into cloth. The wonderful silk cloth produced will be packed and transported along a route known as the Old Silk Road (see pages 108 to 111).

40,000
BCE

# HUNT A MAMMOTH

Travelling thousands of years back in time can be a bumpy ride. You find yourself crash-landing right in the middle of a group of muscular, hairy people. What's more – they're all armed! Every single one of them is holding a wooden spear with a pointed tip that looks very sharp indeed. These hairy people are called Neanderthals – a species of primitive human.

Resist the temptation to push EJECT on your TT handset. It's not you the small hairy hunters are after — it's a mammoth. Mammoths are a type of hairy elephant, with long curved tusks, that are extinct today. You've landed in one of the top Neanderthal mammoth-hunting teams. So, get ready for your first mammoth hunt.

## A MAMMOTH TASK

One of the team hands you a spear and points to the ground. There's a trail of enormous footprints on the ground, and an enormous pile of steaming mammoth poo — sure signs a mammoth is nearby.

When it comes to hunting, a mammoth has all the advantages except one — it's you and the team who have the brains. There are various ways to outwit a mammoth. You could build a huge pit, disguise it with leaves and branches, then herd the mammoth into it. Alternatively, if you find a weak mammoth, use spears, stones or poisoned darts to finish it off.

Today your team is hoping to use the mammoth's own size against it. They plan to drive it into a nearby swamp. Mammoths can grow to over 3 metres tall and weigh over 7,000 kilograms. Their tusks are sharp and can be 3 metres long. This much mammoth is a lot easier to kill once it's floundering in swampy water!

First the team quietly and stealthily surrounds the mammoth, leaving just one gap for it to escape through — right into the muddy swamp. Then, at the team leader's signal, you all charge at the mammoth, shouting, yelling and swinging flaming sticks.

Be careful to keep your footing so you don't get trampled. The panicking mammoth will look for a way out, and if it sees a gap it will make a run for it.

# HUNTING HINTS

Mammoth hunting is risky and difficult, but there are things you can do to give you and your team a greater chance of success:

- Always make sure to keep downwind of a mammoth. That way you can smell the mammoth – and a mammoth is easy to smell – but the mammoth can't smell you.

- Make as little noise as possible when closing in on a mammoth. Move slowly and tread very carefully. Keep your weight on your back foot while you use your front foot to check for sticks or anything else that might make a noise. Only move your weight on to your front foot when you're sure you can do so quietly and without tripping.

- Above all, stick with your team. One on one, you wouldn't stand a chance against a mammoth. It's huge – a fully grown mammoth weighs over 150 times more than you do.

If the mammoth stops feeding, raises its trunk high above its head, and swivels it about, it's bad news. Your mammoth has nostrils at the end of its trunk, and those nostrils may have picked up your scent.

- If you are sure your mammoth has spotted you – don't panic. Top mammoth hunters never panic. Instead, freeze. Your mammoth may never have seen a human before, and it may not know what you're planning. If you stay still your mammoth might relax and go back to its feeding, because feeding was probably a full-time job for a mammoth. Like elephants, mammoths may have needed to feed for up to 18 hours a day.

2500
BCE

## HOW TO ...

# MAKE PAPYRUS IN ANCIENT EGYPT

You've landed behind a thick clump of reeds beside the river Nile in Egypt. No one has spotted you – and make sure you keep it that way, because what you're about to see is a closely guarded secret. It is 2500 BCE, and the ancient Egyptians are the only people in the whole world who have worked out how to make writing scrolls from a special kind of reed called papyrus. They make a lot of money selling these scrolls, and they don't want anyone else to know how they make them. If they see you they might think you're a spy, and who knows what they'll do to you?

## WARNING

You might want to look out for crocodiles as well. They are very common in this part of the world and like nothing more than lurking in reeds, just like the ones you are hiding in.

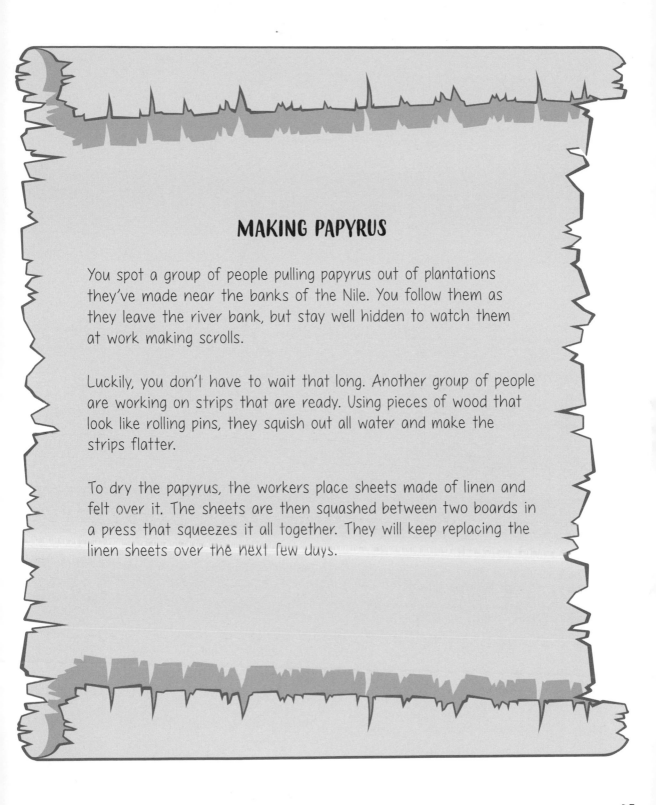

# MAKING PAPYRUS

You spot a group of people pulling papyrus out of plantations they've made near the banks of the Nile. You follow them as they leave the river bank, but stay well hidden to watch them at work making scrolls.

Luckily, you don't have to wait that long. Another group of people are working on strips that are ready. Using pieces of wood that look like rolling pins, they squish out all water and make the strips flatter.

To dry the papyrus, the workers place sheets made of linen and felt over it. The sheets are then squashed between two boards in a press that squeezes it all together. They will keep replacing the linen sheets over the next few days.

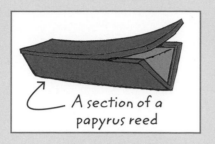

A section of a papyrus reed

Papyrus reeds have a tough outside layer that is peeled off. The workers keep this bit and use it to make other things, like baskets and sandals.

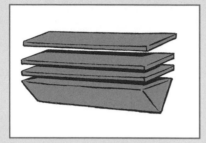

Inside there is a sticky stalk bit that they slice into strips. They bash these strips flat with heavy blocks of wood and then soak them in water from the river for up to three days.

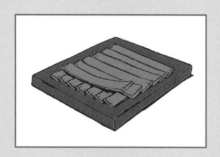

Next, they start laying the strips out, each one overlapping the one before it a tiny bit. The first layer is horizontal, then they add a vertical layer on top. The strips contain a natural sticky gum, so they glue themselves together as they dry.

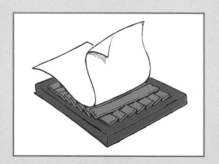

You see a pile of finished papyrus being joined together, end to end, to make a big roll, about 30 metres long. You also see the man who's joining them look up. He's spotted you – it's time to go.

# JOIN THE AMERICAN GOLD RUSH

**1850 CE**

Splash! The good news is you have landed in the state of California, on the west coast of the USA. The bad news is you have landed in a river. In front of you is a man holding a pan half in, half out of the water, and he is swirling about a bit of muck and silt. The man is staring down at it very hard.

All of a sudden he gives a big shout, throws his hat in the air – and that's when you see that there is something interesting in the pan after all. A small chunk of metal is glittering in the silt at the bottom of his pan. Gold!

## THE FORTY-NINERS

When he has stopped jumping for joy, he introduces himself as Nathaniel. Gold was discovered in this river in March 1848. At first people didn't believe the news – they thought it was just a government scheme to get folks to move west to California from their comfortable homes in the east. Now thousands of people have rushed here to strike it rich.

They call it 'gold fever'. People seem to have gone crazy – obsessed with the idea of finding gold. The people that came here are called 'Forty-niners' because they arrived in 1849. Since then, new towns have been springing up.

# A FLASH IN THE PAN

Your friend is one of the lucky Forty-niners. He came early when there was still gold to be had. Back then he was panning nearly $100 a day. He brought along his whole family, selling everything they had to get here — their house, their furniture, even their dog. They travelled over 2,000 miles across the continent in boiling heat.

Now, Nathaniel's noticed he is finding far less gold. It's running out. Today's find was his first find in weeks. But more people are arriving every day. They spend up to ten hours a day standing in freezing water panning for gold, but find nothing.

## MAKING MONEY

Along with all the people looking for gold, known as 'prospectors', others have arrived — merchants and con men. They are hated. They make their money by buying up every bit of gold-panning equipment in the area, and then selling it at many times the original price. Others charge huge amounts for food and supplies. Those prospectors who do not find gold can't afford food at these incredible prices — some even starve to death.

# PANNING FOR GOLD

Nathaniel is not too downcast. One Forty-niner pulled a nugget out of this river the size of a turkey egg – right where you are standing, he tells you. He offers you a pan, and shows you how to pan for gold.

**1** Fill your pan about half full with the mixture of dirt, gravel and silt that has collected at the banks of the river.

**2** Gently put your pan beneath the surface and fill it with water. Take it out and break up all the muddy clumps with your hands to loosen all the silt – and perhaps gold.

**3** Drain away some of the water and take out twigs and lumps of rock. Tip the pan beneath the surface of the water gently to fill the pan again.

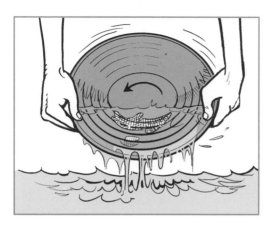

**4** Now swirl the pan near the surface of the water. Gold is heavy, so this should make it sink towards the bottom. Be gentle and take care not to slosh any silt out of your pan.

**5** As you keep shaking, the lighter silt rises up. Lift the pan out of the water, and tilt the front down. Water will run off the edge of the pan, taking the lighter silt at the top with it. Any gold should be in the bottom of the pan.

You keep swirling and tipping away the silt for what feels like ages. Nathaniel finishes his pan and fills up to start again. You are about to do the same when ... you see it: something glinting in the bottom of the pan. It might not be the size of a turkey egg, but you've done it – you've struck gold.

Unfortunately, Nathaniel reminds you that he has staked a claim to this bit of river. That means the gold is his. Instead, he gives you a slice of his wife's homemade pie – hmmm ...

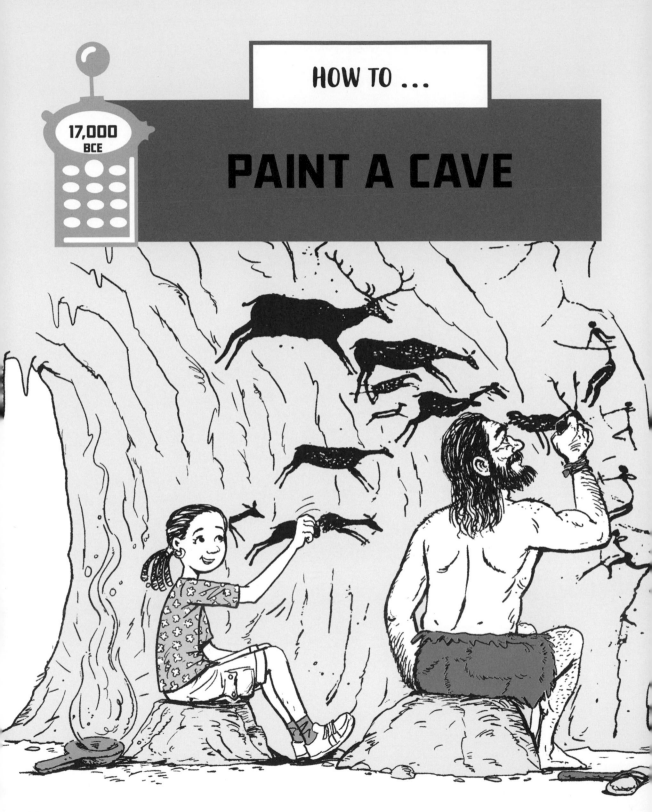

It's pitch dark; you can't see a thing, and you have no idea where you've landed. Luckily, all TT handsets are equipped with an emergency illuminator switch. You press it, and at once the room is flooded with light. But it's not a room at all. You are inside an enormous cave, and there's an incredible painting of two huge white bulls on the wall in front of you.

You walk further on and see that wall after wall is covered in paintings of huge animals. Up ahead you see light glimmering. Follow the light, and you find yourself in another huge cave, about 30 metres long. There's someone in there, hard at work, sketching the outline of a leaping horse across the cave wall.

You're in the Lascaux Cave, in the Pyrenees, France – a series of caves and tunnels filled with what will become some of the most famous Stone Age cave paintings in the world. The gallery you're in right now is known as the Painted Gallery, and has walls 3.5 metres high.

## SHEDDING SOME LIGHT

The glimmering is coming from a flat sandstone lamp with a hollowed out dip at one end. The artist has filled this dip with something that is burning brightly enough for you to see what he is doing.

The paintings you have seen are all in browns, blacks, reds and greys. The artist is using paints made from minerals and natural substances. Some rocks contain a lot of 'iron oxide'; this substance gives a rusty red colour. Rocks containing something called 'manganese oxide' give a strong black colour. The artist shows you how he grinds them down to a powder and mixes them with either water or grease to make them easier to apply to the cave walls.

## PAINT YOUR OWN CAVE

The artist hands you his painting implement and now it's your turn to have a go at painting a mammoth.

### YOU WILL NEED:

- paper • a pencil • wax crayons
- a cup of strong cold tea • a large paintbrush

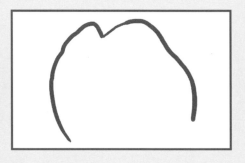

**1** First draw the mammoth's outline – with a hump for its head and one for its back – it should look like a fat 'M' shape.

**2** Add the bottom of the mammoth's trunk and its mouth. Don't forget the shaggy fur.

**3** Next, draw the ears, eye and tusks ...

**4** ... and some legs.

**5** Using a large paintbrush, cover your paper with cold tea to give it that authentic ancient-cave look. You should still be able to see your drawing through the tea. Don't worry if your paper wrinkles.

**6** Now you're ready to go over your mammoth in wax crayons. The cave painters didn't have a lot of colours to choose from, so stick to reds, orangey-yellows, browns and blacks for an authentic look.

## TOP TIP

Why not think bigger? Get hold of some lining paper for walls and create a long row of animals along one wall of your bedroom. Add lots of stick men holding spears. Don't draw straight on your walls. You may think it's the best way to relive your cave-painting experience, but chances are your mum will get angrier than a mammoth with a spear in its side.

# DEFEND A MEDIEVAL CASTLE

**1282 CE**

You land with a jolt to find yourself balancing precariously on the high wall of Hawarden Castle in Wales. A soldier grabs you down from the wall, but as you start to thank him, you see a pretty scary sight. The castle, which stands on top of a hill, is under siege. The sword-wielding army of a Welsh prince named Dafydd ap Gruffudd ap Llywelyn has surrounded the castle and is attacking relentlessly.

The soldier who grabbed you tells you that he and his fellow soldiers have been fighting the Welsh for many years – since 1067, in fact. The Normans had successfully conquered the English in 1066 at the Battle of Hastings. They then built castles along the border with Wales, but failed to completely conquer the Welsh. This was due to the mountainous, rugged terrain of Wales and to the fierce fighting of the Welsh.

## THE CALL TO ARMS

It's only recently, in 1277 under the rule of King Edward I, that the conquest of Wales was completed. To cement his victory and maintain control of the land, Edward has built several massive stone castles, including this one. Unfortunately, the Welsh are still angry and keep revolting against the invaders. This is their strongest revolt yet.

The soldier thrusts a crossbow into your hands and tells you to prepare for battle. To your left and right are men armed with bows and arrows, crossbows, or leather pouches filled with stones. As the attacking army advances up the hill, the soldier quickly shows you how to use the shape of the wall to your advantage.

The wall has been built with a series of square holes cut into the top of it, called 'crenellations'. The English soldiers can shoot their arrows through these holes, and then retreat behind the cover of the wall. In the walls of the towers there are also thin windows, known as 'arrow loops', which are just the right size to shoot arrows through, but very difficult for the attackers down below to aim at.

In between firing arrows, the soldier tells you that this attack has been going on for many days. Roger of Clifford holds this castle and the surrounding settlements for the King. He has retreated with his family and servants into the 'keep' — that is the inner part of the castle behind you and the strong castle walls.

The keep is the safest place to be. Inside the keep there is enough food, water and provisions stored to keep them going for weeks.

Your friend praises the great work you're doing with the crossbow, but points out that the Welsh army is coming up the hill towards the castle's battlements with a nasty-looking battering ram. They plan to break down the heavy wooden gates. You look worried, but he doesn't seem too concerned. He points to the battlements above the gatehouse, where an enormous cauldron of water is being heated over a fire. In the floor beneath are the delightfully named 'Murder Holes', through which the cauldron will be emptied. As soon as the attackers get too close, they are going to get a very nasty scalding.

Next, however, the Welsh army starts using massive catapults, called 'trebuchets', to launch boulders into the outer walls. Soon you see enemy soldiers swarming into the castle through the huge holes that the boulders have made. You decide it's all getting a bit too close for comfort, and as an arrow whizzes past your ear, you decide it's time to hit EJECT and head home.

# MAKE A MEDIEVAL HELMET

Have a go at making your own medieval helmet. Then you will always have it handy for the next time you are under siege.

## YOU WILL NEED:

- a large piece of silver card • scissors • sticky tape
- a pencil • a ruler • some string • a glass jam jar

**1**  Measure around your head using the piece of string. To do this, hold your string at one end against your forehead, 2 cm above your eyebrows, and wrap the rest of it around your head until the length of the string touches the end. Keep hold of the string at the point where it meets the loose end and measure from that point to the end using your ruler. Make a note of the length of the string.

**2**  Take your card and lay it down lengthwise in front of you, silver side down. Measure from the left edge of your card the length you noted down and mark it clearly.

**3**  Measure and mark 3 cm up from the edge of the card nearest you. Use this mark to draw a rectangle 3 cm by (the length of your string). Add an extra 5 cm to the right of your rectangle. This will be used to fasten your helmet.

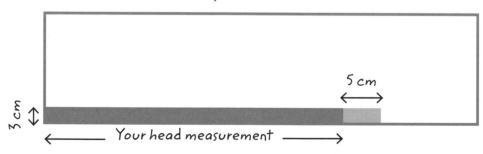

**4**  Measure and mark 25 cm up from the 3 cm line. Divide this up into five equal rectangles (ignoring the 5 cm fastener).

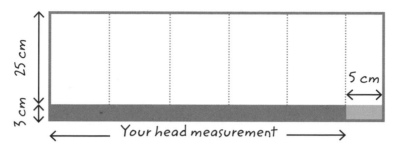

**5**  Next, take your ruler and place it along the line you have drawn furthest from the bottom of your card. Measure and mark the midpoint of each of the five rectangles.

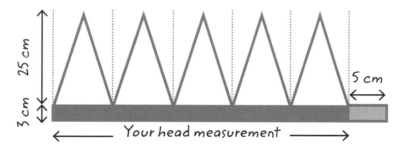

**6**  Now use your ruler to draw lines linking the corners of each rectangle along the 3 cm line up to the midpoints of the rectangles along the 25 cm line. This will give you five triangle shapes. Cut out your helmet as shown above, putting your leftover card to one side for later.

**7**  Next, roll your cut-out into a tall crown shape, silver side out.

**8**  Use the 5 cm tab to fasten your helmet by making sure it overlaps fully. Secure this with sticky tape.

**9** Take your jam jar and place it open side down onto the plain side of your leftover card. Draw around it using a pencil and cut out the circle.

**10** Mark the mid point of your circle and then cut a single line from the edge of the circle to the mid point. Bend your circle of card into a cone shape and secure this with tape.

**11** Take some leftover card and draw a rectangle measuring 20 cm by 3 cm and cut it out. This will be your nosepiece.

**12** Take your helmet and carefully bend in the triangles until they meet in the middle to make a tall dome shape. Stick these together using tape. Don't worry if this looks messy – you won't be able to see this when you've finished.

**13** Use more tape to stick your cone shape to the top of your helmet. It should cover up the joined tops of your triangles and make your helmet more secure.

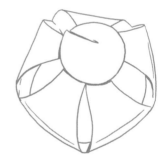

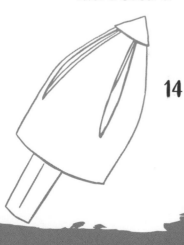

**14** Your helmet is almost finished. Take the nose piece and bend it in half lengthwise so that the two plain edges meet. Unfold it again. This should have made a ridge down the middle. Stick this to the inside of your helmet using sticky tape.

# HOW TO ...

# COMPETE AT THE ANCIENT OLYMPICS

You have landed on a running track in a huge stadium, which is packed with noisy spectators on all sides. It's day one of the ancient Olympiad, the biggest festival in ancient Greece, celebrated in honour of Zeus, king of the Greek gods.

Just like the Olympics in modern times, the Olympiad is held every four years, but always here at Olympia. The festival is considered so important that wars between cities are stopped so that the athletes can travel safely to the games.

## FIGHTING FIT

Nervously, you line up with a group of boys who are about your age and size. They're all warming up for a 192-metre sprint from one end of the stadium to the other.

The ancient Greeks think being fit and healthy is very important. All boys in ancient Greece do a lot of athletic training, and these are the cream of the crop. They've been training hard for months in a place called the *palaestra*, the wrestling school. They have been eating healthily and working hard – which means you're up against some tough competition.

As you are waiting for the starter's orders, follow these top tips:

- Try not to let the butterflies in your stomach bother you. They'll go as soon as you start running. It's caused by your body producing a chemical called 'adrenaline'. This is completely natural and will give you a burst of speed across the stadium.

- Don't worry about not having your running shoes with you. Take a look around. No one else is wearing any - in fact they aren't wearing anything at all! Ancient Greek men and boys trained and competed completely naked. So strip off and get ready to run.

- Try to block out the roaring crowd and go through the race in your head. Imagine yourself being super-speedy and think how good you'll feel when you cross that finishing line first.

## WHAT NEXT?

The downside is that if you win you shouldn't expect a medal. Ancient Greeks didn't do medals. Winners get a crown made out of olive branches.

The good bit is Olympic winners are celebrities and are greeted by cheering crowds when they return home to their towns and cities. In the meantime, while you are in Olympia you can expect some nice free meals and front-row seats at the theatre. You may even get a statue built in your honour.

# WHILE YOU WAIT

If you win any of the races, you'll have to hang around for your prize, because the ancient Olympiad goes on for five days and the prizes are all given out at the end.

Here are a few things you can do while you're waiting:

- What better way to while away the hours than taking in a chariot race or two? There are two- and four-horse events, as well as a cart-and-mule race. Chariot races are very exciting, with up to 40 chariots jostling for first place during the 12 laps. You might not want to sit in the front row for this one, though. Crashes are common and you don't want to get trampled by a runaway horse.

- For some seriously tough sport, why not watch some boxing? The boxers don't wear gloves like modern boxers, they just wrap bits of leather round their hands, leaving their fingers sticking out.

The boxing matches don't have rounds; each fight continues until someone gives up or loses consciousness. Watch out for a man named Theagenes of Thasos – he is tipped to be this year's winner. At the age of nine, he was so strong that he managed to tear a bronze statue of a god off its base and carry it home.

## GIRLS ALLOWED

Although girls weren't allowed to compete in the ancient Olympic Games, a separate festival in honour of Zeus' wife, Hera, was held here in Olympia. It was called the *Heraia* and took place every four years, too. The *Heraia* was the ancient Greek girls' chance to show off their running skills. To compete, girls wore tunics cut just above the knee and draped over their left shoulder.

**70 MILLION BCE**

# TACKLE A T. REX

The sound of something large and angry crashing through the undergrowth fills your ears. Checking your TT handset, you find you have travelled back over 70 million years. You are standing in a steamy forest of towering conifer, palm and magnolia trees, in an area now known as Hell Creek in Montana, USA. Unfortunately, at the time you have arrived this area is also Dinosaur Central! Suddenly, you're face to face – well, your face to its knee – with one of the most ferocious and terrifying dinosaurs in history ... *Tyrannosaurus Rex*.

## DOS AND DON'TS

To minimize your chances of ending up as a *Tyrannosaurus Rex's* lunch, here are some life-saving precautions to take:

**DON'T** try to hide. a *Tyrannosaurus Rex* has very good, all-round eyesight and a brilliant sense of smell. It will sniff you out very quickly.

**DO** avoid a *Tyrannosaurus Rex's* gnashers. His powerful jaws are lined with up to 60 bone-crunching teeth. Bite marks found on the fossils of other dinosaurs show that a *Tyrannosaurus Rex* can open its massive mouth wide enough to bite off as much as 70 kilograms of meat in one go — which is substantially more than the whole of you!

**DON'T** let the *Tyrannosaurus Rex* tread on you. A fully grown *Tyrannosaurus Rex* is massive — up to 14 metres long, 6 metres tall and weighing around 7 tonnes. Even a *Tyrannosaurus Rex* teenager weighs around 3 tonnes.

**DON'T** be tempted to stand and fight. Even though, compared to its back limbs, a *Tyrannosaurus Rex's* front limbs are tiny, you wouldn't stand a chance in a boxing match. Its claws pack a powerful punch. Some dinosaur experts think a *Tyrannosaurus Rex* used its 'arms' for holding struggling prey – and you don't want to prove them right

**DO** make a run for it. A *Tyrannosaurus Rex* walks on its two powerful back legs but can't run very fast. It simply doesn't have the muscle power. Its maximum speed is about 18 kilometres per hour, but it can't keep that up for very long.

**DO** look out for a dinosaur with a mouth like a duck's bill and stay as far away from it as you can. This is an *Edmontosaurus*, a *Tyrannosaurus Rex's* favourite food.

# BUILD A VIKING LONGSHIP

**832 CE**

You've touched down on the coast of Norway during the age of the Vikings. The Vikings are explorers, warriors and merchants who mainly live in what is now known as Scandinavia.

You seem to be in a long hut, surrounded by several women who are hard at work sewing together pieces of linen to make a large, square shape. One of them hands you a needle and thread. At that moment, a huge man walks into the hut.

The man, who is called Olaf, takes you outside, where dozens of people are busy building a magnificent ship. It is almost ready to set sail. As he walks you round, Olaf tells you exactly what the workers have done so you can try and build your own.

Longships can be as long as 30 metres, so you will need to chop down a very tall tree to form the ship's keel – the long central piece that runs all the way along the bottom of the ship. Attach large curved pieces of wood to each end of the keel to form the front and back of the ship, known as the bow and the stern.

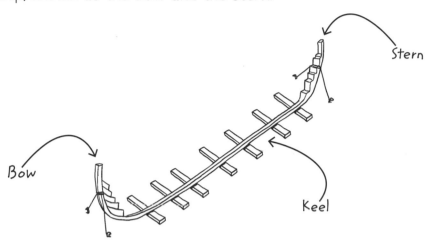

Stern

Bow

Keel

Fix support planks, called 'ribs' and 'crossbeams', at right angles to the keel. Take some sturdy side planks and attach them from the bow to the stern to form the sides and bottom of the ship. Each plank should overlap the one below it and be fixed in place with iron rivets. Add a large block of wood to support the mast.

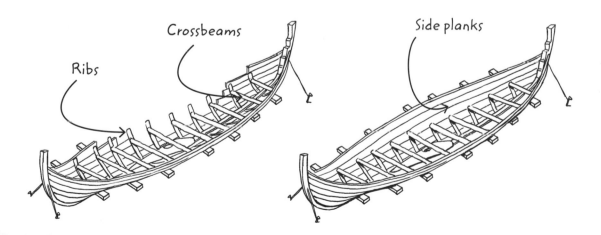

Crossbeams

Side planks

Ribs

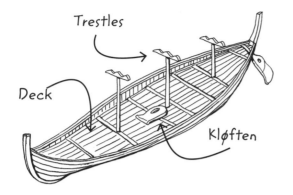

Trestles

Deck

Kløften

Lay smooth planks over the crossbeams to form the deck. Fix a large, fish-shaped piece of wood onto the deck for the mast to slot through. This is called the kløften. Add trestles, to hold the sail when it is lowered.

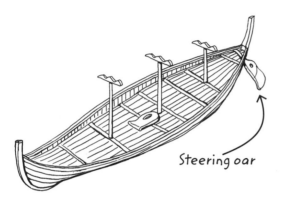

Steering oar

Drill holes in the side of the ship for the long, thin oars to poke through. At the stern of the boat add a large steering oar. Make sure you make some discs of wood that can be slotted over the holes to stop water getting in when the oars aren't being used.

To make your ship seaworthy, you need to 'caulk' it. Get some animal fur and dip it into hot tar. The tar is smelly stuff but it will make your ship waterproof. Push your tar-soaked wads of fur between the planks of the ship, making sure there are no gaps.

Olaf tells you he is going to call his ship the *Sea Dragon*. He leads you to a skilled carpenter who is carving a fearsome dragon's head to mount on the bow of the boat.

He invites you to join his voyage, but the deck looks like it will be quite crowded with all those big strong Vikings on board. What's more, pulling the ship's heavy oars doesn't look like fun. So you wave them off on their way from the shore, and hit the EJECT button.

# HOW TO ...

# ACT IN A SHAKESPEAREAN PLAY

In front of you appears a man with a pointy beard and a twirly moustache. He is pacing around, tugging at his hair and muttering to himself. You have landed backstage at the Globe theatre, in London, and this is William Shakespeare, who will become probably the most famous playwright in history.

Right now, however, Shakespeare's in trouble. Halfway through a performance of his new play, one of his actors has rushed offstage. The boy has a green face and he's holding his stomach and groaning about eating one too many eel pies.

## THE SHOW MUST GO ON

Just then Will spots you and decides you'd be the perfect replacement. Before you know it, he's shoving a script in your hand and giving you a few acting tips:

- Speak up. The audience sitting up in the highest gallery are a long way away. If you breathe in from just above your belly button and fill this bit up with air, your voice will be much stronger and travel much further without you needing to shout.

- Speak clearly. Pronounce your words more precisely than you would normally. If you talk too quickly or slur your words, the audience won't be able to understand you and will get bored.

- Look around. The Globe theatre is circular and has the audience on three sides of the stage, so you need to move your body so you can be seen by everyone.

If you follow these tips, hopefully the 3,000-strong audience won't get bored. If they do, watch out. Rowdy Elizabethan audiences will throw things. If you see any food flying through the air – duck, or you could get a rotten turnip in your face.

# HOW TO STAGE A FIGHT

William Shakespeare has written plays about love, war, witches, murders, ghosts and shipwrecks – anything to keep his audience interested. He loves to write about fights. The play is *Macbeth* and has a great fight scene. William quickly tells you how to stage a fight so you can take part in the play on stage right now.

Every single move in a stage fight is planned out and rehearsed over and over again. Read his tips and practise with a friend:

**1** Arm yourselves. Remember that the whole point of your stage fight is that neither of you gets hurt. So choose your weapons carefully. The long cardboard tubes you get in wrapping paper are ideal.

**2** Decide why you are fighting. This will provide drama. One of you perhaps is the king and the other is wanting to steal his throne, or you could be pirates fighting over a pot of gold.

**3**   Find a good place to rehearse, like a garden or park; then you can start to create your fight.

**4**   Be entertaining. If you both just go whack, whack, whack with the swords it will be boring. Swing round things. Jump off things. Use props: maybe one of you can drop your sword and be forced to use something else to fight with. Be inventive.

**5**   Once you have worked out your moves, rehearse them slowly at first until you are sure you both know them in the right order. Then speed them up, and gradually work the fight up to full speed.

## TOP TIP

Don't forget the sound effects. Grunts, gasps and shouts are all good. To make it sound really authentic, say things like "Alack!" or "I'm slain". Dying scenes should be as long and drawn out as possible.

## HOW TO ...

# WALK ON THE MOON

**1969 CE**

No sooner have your feet touched the ground than they leave it again. Somewhat alarmed, you find yourself floating. You're in some kind of spacecraft. You're weightless and confused. Suddenly you see something outside a window – a huge round something, a something you've seen almost every night of your life, but never this close – the Moon.

The Moon is so vast and so near, you feel you could almost reach out and touch it. You're on the Lunar Module 'Eagle', which has been launched from the spacecraft *Columbia*. It is a weird-looking contraption – silver, yellow and orange with legs – and it is heading for touchdown on the Moon.

On board with you are two astronauts – Neil Armstrong and Buzz Aldrin – and they're about to become the first people to set foot on the Moon.

## MOON WALKING FOR BEGINNERS

Walking on the Moon takes a bit of getting used to. Here are some things to watch out for:

- On the Moon you will weigh six times less than you do on Earth because the force of gravity pulling you towards the Moon's surface is less powerful than the force on Earth.

- It is harder to balance on the Moon and you will have to lean forwards slightly more than usual. When you want to stop, it will take you a few steps to do so.

## TOUCHDOWN

You're lucky to be walking on the Moon at all. You and the astronauts had to dodge around lots of huge boulders and a big crater before you found a landing place.

Buzz takes a shine to jogging – well, bounding – on the Moon, but you notice that the moon dust doesn't scatter itself randomly like dust does on Earth. Moon dust travels neatly and precisely, so the prints left by his boots are very clear. As there's no wind, rain or creatures on the Moon, the footprints will probably still be very clear millions of years from now.

Buzz and Neil struggle to plant the US flag on the Moon's surface. They can't dig its pole very far into the ground, so it won't stay upright. In fact, it falls over anyway when you take off and head back to *Columbia*.

## BACK ON BOARD *COLUMBIA*

In the weightless conditions back on *Columbia*, you have time to find out a few things about life in space.

- Eating is tricky. You have to strap your meal tray to one of your legs when you eat. The things on the tray have got rubber grips to stop them floating off. The food comes in little vacuum packs, but once you open a pack, you have to grab hold of the food with your hand quickly, or jab a fork into it to stop it escaping. You have to suck your drinks out of a tube.

- One of the astronauts warns you to strap yourself to the toilet seat, but he doesn't warn you about the noise the toilet makes. It's the waste being sucked away to somewhere where it won't float back out again.

- Floating about, turning somersaults and doing back flips inside the spacecraft is extremely good fun, but being sick in weightless conditions is extremely not.

- When you take a space nap, you have to tie yourself down first. There's a lot of highly sensitive equipment around, and one bad dream and one flailing arm in the wrong place could wreck the whole space mission.

# GRADUATE FROM GLADIATOR SCHOOL

108 CE

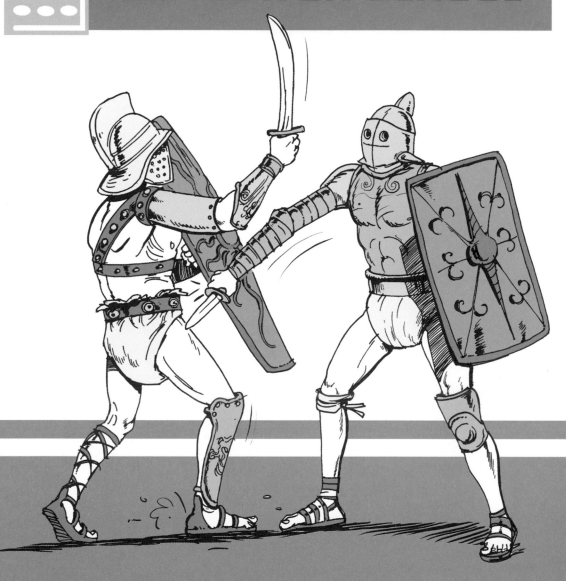

It's just after dawn and you've landed in the training ground of an ancient Roman gladiator school. It's called a *ludus* and is full of sweating, grunting men wearing heavy armour, warming up for a hard day's training.

As you watch, you don't notice an older man approaching. Thinking you are a slave, he gives you a clip around the ear and tells you to get on with your work. He is called Ferox, and he is a *magister*, or trainer, at the school. Quickly, you explain to him that you want to become a gladiator. "It's a tough life," Ferox laughs. "And I should know – I was a famous gladiator myself."

## SLAVES AND CRIMINALS

Most of the gladiators in the *ludus* aren't volunteers. Most of the men and women here are slaves or criminals; others are prisoners of war. They didn't choose to be here, and they can't choose to leave. Gladiators only gain their freedom if they manage to survive several years of fighting.

It's not all bad. At the *ludus*, the gladiators are looked after well, and given food and medical treatment when they need it. They are very competitive and strive to work their way up grades called *paloi* to become the *primus palus* – the best and most respected gladiator in the *ludus*. A *primus palus* can become as famous as a premiership footballer is today.

# IN THE ARENA

Today there is going to be a big gladiatorial contest in the arena, and Ferox says you can come along to help. As you enter the arena, the roar of 50,000 spectators almost shatters your eardrums. The organizer of the contest smiles and waves at the crowd from his chariot, which is part of the parade. Behind him come the gladiators and the slaves who carry their armour, and then you. The man whose armour you are carrying used to be a soldier, but he was captured during a battle. For three years he has fought as a gladiator, and today is his last contest. If he survives he'll be free.

You follow your gladiator down a passage to a room beneath the arena. It's a dark, terrifying place down here. You hear the crowd above baying for blood. Your gladiator has chosen a curved sword, a shield, leg armour, and a helmet. He prefers to dress lightly so he can move around more easily.

Suddenly, a trap door opens above you. You hear the roar of the crowd get louder. Your gladiator's last fight is going to be with what looks like a very fierce gladiator who hasn't lost a fight yet. You hit EJECT – things are about to get messy.

# PLAY *PRIMUS PALUS*

Back in the future, it's a good idea to stay fighting fit in case you land back in the arena when you are least expecting it. Find an open space, like a large garden or park, set up this four-station obstacle course and train with your friends. Who will be *primus palus* - the greatest gladiator of all?

## YOU WILL NEED:

- at least two players • a large old bed sheet (one that can get muddy without anyone getting cross) • large stones
- six empty cereal boxes • a tennis ball • a tablespoon
- a bucket • a quoit or beanbag • a stopwatch

## OBSTACLE ONE
Lay out your sheet and place large stones on each corner to anchor it down. Put more along two opposite sides to hold it down, leaving enough slack for 'gladiators' to scramble beneath it.

## OBSTACLE TWO
Stand the six cereal boxes in a straight line about 50 centimetres apart. If it is a windy day, fill the boxes with stones. This 'standing jump sequence' is designed to strengthen your legs and improve balance. Competitors need to jump with both feet together over each box without taking an extra step or knocking the boxes over. If they do, they have to start again at the beginning.

## OBSTACLE THREE

Place the spoon and tennis ball on the ground and the bucket 10 metres away from them. This obstacle is a test of both co-ordination and instinct. Walk as fast as you can towards the bucket, balancing the tennis ball on the spoon. If the ball is dropped you need to start again. When you reach the bucket you need to turn around so your back is to the bucket, and attempt to throw the ball over your head and into the bucket using the spoon.

## OBSTACLE FOUR

Place the quoit or beanbag next to the bucket used in Obstacle Three. When a gladiator has successfully thrown the ball into the bucket, he must balance the beanbag or quoit on top of his head and run backwards along the length of the course to the start without dropping it.

## AND THE WINNER IS ...

Once you have set up your course and each of the players understands what to do at the various obstacles, the game can begin. Take turns at completing the course, one at a time. Have a few practice goes each, to work out your tactics. Then, when everyone is ready, take your stopwatch and time each gladiator completing the course. The fastest is the winner and takes the title *primus palus*.

## TOP TIP

Every gladiator has different strengths. Time each event separately to find out who is the best at each one.

**1940 CE**

# SURVIVE THE BLITZ IN BRITAIN

The moment you land, you notice your TT handset is flashing. Something is very wrong. A loud siren starts wailing. It's an air-raid warning and you need to get to shelter fast. The trouble is you can't see a thing, not even your hand in front of your face. You press the Illuminator switch on your TT handset, but straight away someone yells, "PUT THAT LIGHT OUT!"

It's 1940 and you've landed in the middle of the 'Blitz'. The Blitz is the name people are giving to a period during World War Two, when night after night, German planes drop bombs on cities all over Britain.

## THE BLACKOUT

The siren is still blaring and you hear the whistling noise of a bomb dropping to the ground. There is a flash of light and the deafening sound of the explosion. A woman grabs your hand and pulls you through a door and down some steps. There is light down here and you can see where you are. You're in a London Underground train station, packed with people sheltering from a night-time bombing raid on the city.

The woman who grabbed you is called Sylvia. Her husband is away fighting. She apologizes for shouting at you but warns you that you can get in a lot of trouble for showing a light during a 'blackout'. During a blackout everyone has to cover up their windows with thick black curtains just before sunset. The streetlamps are shaded so they let out only a tiny bit of light, and even car headlights point downward and shine through black slits. The government hopes the darkness will make it impossible for the pilots of German bombers to target Britain's cities from the air.

# GOING UNDERGROUND

The station is dirty, with mice scrabbling around. It smells because the toilets are closed and people are having to use buckets instead. But it is the safest place to be. Sylvia explains that at the beginning of the war, the government banned people from sheltering down here. She would just buy a ticket to travel on the Underground, and only come up when the 'all-clear' sirens sounded to tell people the bombers had gone. Now over 200,000 people take cover in stations all over London. There are proper public shelters, but not enough for everyone, and Sylvia doesn't have a garden in which to build a home-made shelter called an 'Anderson shelter'.

Above your head, you can still hear the bombs exploding, and every so often the bench you are sitting on shakes. Sylvia is worried about what she will find when the air raid ends. Last week, one family in her street returned from the shelter to find a heap of rubble where their house used to be.

# BOMBS IN THE BLITZ

Sylvia tells you the German planes overhead are dropping two kinds of bombs:

**1.** Fire bombs, known as 'incendiary bombs'. The Germans drop these first, in clusters. The bombs are small, but full of chemicals, and burst into flames wherever they land. They cause lots of damage and create light for the pilots to see where to drop the rest of their bombs.

**2.** High explosive bombs – packed with explosives. Most of these explode on impact, destroying the buildings around them. Others have timers on them, and explode hours later, without any warning. Army bomb disposal experts try to disarm them, but it's dangerous work and many are killed.

Sylvia tells you that last week, on November 14th 1940, German bombers dropped around 500 tonnes of bombs on the city of Coventry near Birmingham, England. This killed 568 people and injured over 1,000. Over 60,000 buildings were destroyed.

## BEATING THE BLITZ BLUES

- Bring earplugs. If you thought your dad's snoring was bad, an air raid is much worse. The wail of the sirens, the thump of exploding bombs, and the crashing as buildings collapse is terrifying. To keep everyone's spirits up and drown out the sound of the bombs, why not try singing?

- Bring something to do. During a raid, you can be in the shelter for a long time. Sylvia is knitting, but you could try a board game, or a pack of cards.

- Don't go out after sunset unless you have to. The blackout has caused chaos on the roads. Nobody can see where they are going. People bump into lampposts, fall off bridges and cars have crashed into canals.

- Bring a snack. Sadly, sweets and other foods are in short supply. The government controls how much food people can have – this is called 'rationing'.

- Get evacuated – lots of children have been sent to the countryside to live with families away from the bombs. Sylvia has two daughters who have been evacuated to Wales.

**1500 BCE**

# LEAP A MINOAN BULL

It's hot, there's a sparkly sea, olive trees, and green hills – and you realize you have landed on the beautiful island of Crete, the largest of the Greek Islands. What you don't know is that you are about to witness one of the most spectacular and dangerous sports of all time. It is a sport that tests not only strength, speed and agility, but also courage – or stupidity, depending on how you look at it.

A boy wearing a tunic approaches and asks if you'd like to follow him. He is a Minoan, a member of the great civilization that live on Crete and on islands all around the Aegean Sea in 1500 BCE.

He leads you to the edge of a field, where you see an enormous, angry bull scratching at the ground with one of its hooves. In front of it stands a young man who seems to be taunting it, wanting the bull to charge at him. The man is known as a 'leaper', and what he wants to do is leap over the bull in a sport that is part dance, part acrobatics and totally crazy.

## WARNING

Leaping real bulls is something that should be left in the past. Time travellers should never attempt to leap a bull. You could get yourself badly injured or killed.

# THE BULL LEAPER

You watch the bull lunge towards the leaper. Amazingly, instead of running away, the young man stands still. As the bull reaches him, the leaper reaches out and grabs its horns. Immediately, the bull tosses back his head, throwing the man into the air and over his back. The leaper then lets go of the horns and lands expertly on both feet on top of the bull's back. From here, he leaps into the air, performing a perfect somersault, and lands safely behind the bull.

Bulls are very important to the Minoan people. They are called 'Minoan' after a king from long ago named Minos. Legend has it that King Minos built a vast maze to contain a monster that was half man and half bull. This monster was called the Minotaur.

The Minotaur terrorized the island and had to be fed with human flesh until it was eventually killed by a brave hero from Athens named Theseus.

## MEGA MISTAKE

As you watch the leaper you begin to appreciate the beauty of the sport. It's graceful and gymnastic, and the leapers seem extremely brave. Perhaps you have been watching for too long, as one of the leapers asks you if you would like a turn. Before you know it, you are face to face with the biggest and angriest bull of all. Having been leapt over so many times, he looks ready to trample someone.

As the bull is thundering closer and closer, you decide this is not the time to try a new sport, and that it would make sense to go back to the future and get some practice first. So, just as you can feel the bull's breath on your cheek, you hit EJECT.

## HOW TO PLAY LEAPING BULLS

To practise your bull-leaping skills in a park or garden you will need two teams. The following instructions are for teams with three members, but the more the merrier.

Measure out a course 24 metres long, with a clearly marked start and finishing line. (The course will need to be longer if you have more than three people in a team.)

Each team has one 'leaper' and the rest of its members are 'bulls'. The bulls in each team line up along the length of the course, Team A standing 5 metres away from Team B. The first bull in each team stands about 4 metres from the starting line and the second bull stands 4 metres further along the course and so on.

All the bulls must stand side-on to the finish line. They bend over, putting their elbows on their thighs and tucking their heads into their chests, with their index fingers pointing upwards either side of their head. These are the bulls' horns.

The two leapers stand on the starting line. When the game begins the leapers run forward towards the first bull in their line. They place their hands in the centre of the bull's back and leap over. They repeat this over each of the bulls until they have leapt the last one. The leapers then bend over to become bulls themselves and the first bull in the row becomes the leaper.

Continue until the first leaper has leapt twice, then sprinted to the finish line. The first team with a leaper over the line wins.

*Leap over each bull until you reach the end of the line.*

# MAKE AN EGYPTIAN MUMMY

**1550 BCE**

The room you've just landed in has two people in it, but only one of them is alive – fortunately that's you. The other person is a man lying flat out on a stone slab, looking very, very dead.

Your head is buzzing with questions – who is he, what's he doing there, and – most of all – should I hit EJECT and head home? Just then, a man comes in and he has all the answers. He explains that you've landed in the workshop of an ancient Egyptian embalmer. He is the chief embalmer, and he invites you to stay and help.

His job is making the bodies of dead rich people into mummies, so that they don't rot away inside their bandages. He and his team are about to get started on this one.

## EMBALMING

A word of warning here. Making an Egyptian mummy is not just about wrapping a few bandages around a dead body. A lot of grisly stuff goes on first. So if you're the sort who feels a bit queasy seeing one tiny drop of blood, you'd better toughen up – and fast – or hit EJECT. You decide to stay and the embalmer starts to give you instructions.

**1** Push a long hook up the dead man's nose. This breaks up his brain so that you can pull it out through his nose.

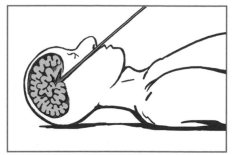

**2** Make a slit in the side of the body and pull out the dead man's internal organs. The embalmer asks if you are sure that you want to do this. Top time travellers are always open to new experiences, so you do – but wish you hadn't. Intestines are long, slimy, stinky and make a lot of squelching noises on their way out.

**3** Place the different organs in separate containers called 'canopic jars' – one for each of the lungs, the liver, the stomach and the intestines.

The embalmer tells you to leave the heart in the body because the dead person needs it in the next world.

Canopic jars

**4** Now cover the whole body with special salt called 'natron'. Stuff small packets of natron inside the body. It will dry the body out, preserve it, and cut down on smells, too.

Natron

**5** The chief embalmer tells you that the body must now be left in the natron for around 40 days, until it is completely dried out. After that time, it will look much thinner and darker. The embalmers will then stuff the body to make it a normal shape again, and sew up the slit you made in the side of the body, ready for wrapping.

## GET WRAPPING

The workshop contains bodies that are at various stages of the mummification process. So now you are told to get to work wrapping a body that was embalmed 40 days earlier. The chief embalmer tells you it's precise, painstaking work. It must be done extremely neatly, because the dead man you are wrapping has a rich and powerful family who are very fussy.

You start by helping to crisscross bandages across the body, starting with the head and then individually wrapping the fingers and toes. The bandages are wrapped in layers, and some of them are decorated with prayers. You're as careful as you can be, but it's tricky work and you get in a bit of a muddle, so they decide to give you the job of sprinkling incense instead.

You sprinkle strong-smelling incense, such as frankincense and myrrh, between each layer of bandages. You pop pieces of jewellery, called amulets, between the layers to ward off evil.

# JOURNEY TO THE UNDERWORLD

While they bandage, the embalmers explain that they believe the dead man's spirit is about to go on a long journey through the 'underworld'. At the end of it he'll meet Osiris, who is the lord of the underworld. If Osiris thinks the man has been good, his spirit will be reunited with his body and he'll live in the 'afterlife'.

People believe that the afterlife will be a better version of the world they live in now. So the dead man's family and friends do all they can to help him on his journey. They write messages and inscriptions on his coffin, and put lots of things in the tomb they think he might need in the afterlife, such as food, clothes, furniture and even underwear. They put replica figures of his servants in his tomb - these are called ushabtis. They put the 'Book of the Dead' in too, a sort of travel guide to the afterlife.

Finally, the chief embalmer puts a mask over the mummy's face. And, because it's hard to tell who's who when they're covered head to foot in bandages, he attaches a label saying who is inside. He doesn't want the mummy to go off to the wrong funeral.

Now you are finished, and it's time to get away from the stinky workshop, so you hit EJECT.

# HOW TO ...

# SURVIVE A VIKING RAID

"Save yourselves, the Vikings are coming!" A cry pierces the morning air as you tumble into the long grass beside a stone wall. You find yourself in a tiny walled settlement beside a monastery, on the coast of Ireland. It's a beautiful spot, if it wasn't for the six Viking longships that have just appeared on the horizon.

The monks and villagers are panicking. They must try to hide the monastery's treasures and get as many people as possible to safety before the ruthless raiders get to the shore.

## BURIED TREASURE

A monk hurrying past you thrusts a golden goblet covered in rubies and emeralds into your hands. "Follow me!" he shouts, and takes you through the monastery to a spot under a tree beside the walls. There you see a freshly dug hole that the other monks are filling with armfuls of gold coins, religious books and silver cups and plates.

The monks hope that by burying their treasure they can stop it falling into the hands of the raiders, who have come to steal it.

In the distance, you can see that the Vikings have landed on the shore. Their longships are designed to sail up shallow rivers and to land on the shores of sandy beaches, making it easy for the men on board to get ashore quickly. Some raiders are on horseback. Planks are pushed out from the ships, which the horses can walk down on to the beach. Other raiders are on foot, shrieking and shouting, as they run towards the settlement. Only a small group of men are left behind to guard the ships.

You spot a group of Vikings killing a herdsman who had been grazing his sheep on the hills above the beach. They herd the sheep back towards their boats and will enjoy eating them later to celebrate the success of their raid.

# THE ENEMY AT THE GATES

A terrible noise reaches your ears. Raiders are using a battering ram to break down the wooden gate to the monastery. As the gate splinters and falls, men wearing helmets that flash in the morning sun pour in through the gap. Mercilessly, they cut down monks and villagers with their big metal swords. Some raiders set fire to the houses, once they have searched them for anything worth stealing.

The abbot, who is in charge of the monastery, pulls you and another monk to one side and tells you to go for help at the fort a kilometre away.

As quickly as you can, you help each other over the wall at the back of the monastery garden. As you look back you can see a long line of women and children who have been rounded up and are being led towards the longships. The Vikings will take them back to Norway, in Scandinavia, and sell them as slaves. You can also see that they have taken the abbot who sent you for help. He will be held to ransom – the church will need to pay a fortune in gold to have him returned safely.

The raiders know they don't have long before help arrives, so they are carrying off anything of any value as quickly as they can. The settlement disappears from view as you run towards the fort. All you can see is a plume of smoke, which is rising from the burning buildings. You wonder if the Vikings have found the hidden treasure beside the wall. If not, it might be worth you looking for it when you go back to the future. It might still be buried there and the local museum would love to have the treasure on display for visitors.

As you reach the fort, you send the monk ahead to plead for help. You have seen enough, and as there is nothing you can do – it's time to hit EJECT!

# HOW TO ...

# WRITE IN HIEROGLYPHS

1450 BCE

You land in what looks like a temple, in front of tall sandstone walls that are engraved with lots of pictures. The pictures, which run up and down the walls in straight lines, are hieroglyphs – one of the very first forms of writing.

You spend a moment trying to work out what all the pictures mean, but even though you recognize some of the shapes – such as birds and snakes – you can't make head or tail of it.

## PICTURE POWER

You look around for someone who might be able to help, and spot a young man with a partly shaven head walking up the steps of the temple. He has a number of papyrus scrolls (see pages 24 to 26) under his arm. Politely, you ask him to help you understand what the hieroglyphs mean. His name is Suten Anu. He is a scribe at the palace of the Pharaoh, the King of Egypt.

Suten tells you that the 'writing' you see on the walls was taught to Egyptians by Thoth, the god of wisdom. Suten believes that the pictures have a power all of their own. It would take years to teach you how to read all of the symbols – there are over 700 of them – but he is happy to give you a few pointers.

# SOUNDS LIKE ...

Suten Anu unrolls one of his papyrus scrolls which contains a list of the symbols most commonly used in the writing. He explains that all of them stand for sounds. He says each sound as he runs his finger down the list.

He indicates matching pictures on the walls and points out the little strokes that appear underneath some of them. He says if you see a stroke under a sound symbol, it means the symbol also stands for an object. For example:

You notice that aren't any punctuation marks, such as full stops or question marks, on his list of symbols. Suten looks at you blankly, and you guess they don't have any.

To make things more confusing, the hieroglyphs can be drawn left to right or right to left, whichever fits the space best.

## CARTOUCHE FOR A KING OR QUEEN

Some hieroglyphs are written in oval frames. These are special ones, known as 'cartouches'. They contain the names of kings and queens. People believe the oval frame protects the royal name. You ask Suten if he could show you how to write your own name in hieroglyphs. He suggests you start by spelling it out with the sound hieroglyphs he showed you earlier, matching the sounds to the letters in your name. Then you attempt to write his name.

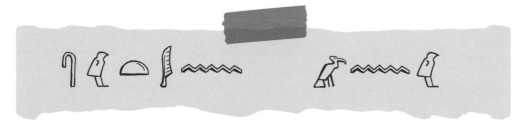

He laughs — it is not quite how he would do it but he thinks that with practice you could make a very good scribe.

## MAKE A CARTOUCHE

Why not practise your hieroglyphic writing by making
a cartouche of your own name?

### YOU WILL NEED

• a sheet of paper and a pencil • self-hardening modelling clay
• a table knife • a rolling pin • a thin knitting needle or skewer
• some paint • paintbrushes • glue

**1** Plan your cartouche on paper first. Use the list on page 90 to pick out all the letters in your name, then write them out on a piece of paper.

**2** Roll out your clay with a rolling pin, until it is 1.5 cm thick.

**3** Cut out an oval shape using a table knife. You can make your cartouche any size you like, but 20 cm by 10 cm should fit most names quite well.

**4** Make the rest of your clay into a long sausage shape by rolling it between your palms. It needs to be long enough so you can attach it all the way around the edge of the oval you cut out.

**5** Next, carve the hieroglyphs that spell out your name into the clay, using a skewer. Do it lightly first, to check that you can fit your name in. Then go over your hieroglyphs again, pressing a bit harder.

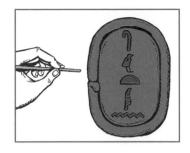

**6** When you have finished, let the clay dry, or bake it following the instructions on the packet.

**7** Paint your cartouche with a coat of yellow paint to make the clay look like sandstone. Then leave it to dry.

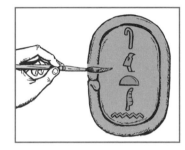

**8** When the yellow paint is completely dry, use a thin paintbrush to paint your hieroglyphs in bold colours.

Display your finished cartouche somewhere in your room to alert your family to your royal status. It might make them treat you like a pharaoh, and that is good — pharaohs were treated like gods!

# INVENT WRITING WITH THE SUMERIANS

**3100 BCE**

You've just touched down in ancient Mesopotamia, an area now known as Iraq. The Sumerians – the name given to the people who lived there in 3100 BCE – are a brainy lot. They are good at building, farming, maths, astronomy, and all sorts of other things. They're extremely good at inventing things, too. Some experts think that they may even have invented the wheel, so keep your eyes peeled for proof.

It might not look like it, but the man sitting down right beside you is busy inventing right now. He's writing. Time travellers will tell you that the Sumerians were the first people in the history of the world known to have used writing. This is a truly historical moment, so sit yourself down and join him.

## THE WRITE STUFF

Even though the Sumerians are very smart, they haven't invented paper. The man hands you a wet clay tablet to write on. There are no pens or pencils in Mesopotamia either, so he lends you one of his spare writing sticks called a 'stylus'. It has a pointed end for making marks in the wet clay.

### WRITE HERE, WRITE NOW

The man tells you the reason he is writing is because people need a way to keep records of the crops they are growing and the things they are making. He is using the very earliest form of Sumerian writing, writing that will change and develop over the next 2,000 years.

He makes the symbol for barley, something Sumerians grow a lot of, by pushing his stylus into the soft clay and drawing lines, like this:

The finished symbol looks a bit like some of the logos you see around in the present, but not like any word you have seen before. The man draws more picture symbols and asks you to guess what each one means (see the answers on page 127).

95

## WRITER'S BLOCKS

Back in the present you will find quite a few clay tablets that have survived from Sumerian times – maybe even the one your friend is working on right now. The reason for this is that all the inventing the Sumerians did made them rich. As a result, people that lived around them grew jealous and attacked the Sumerians, attempting to steal from them. One way they would attack was to burn Sumerian buildings. Inside burning buildings, the clay writing tablets got hard baked, and were preserved for centuries.

## INVENT YOUR OWN WRITING

Why not try your hand at creating your own Sumerian-style symbols for things around today that you like best?

### YOU WILL NEED:

- a pencil • some paper • a sharp stick
- some modelling clay • a rolling pin • an oven

Use the pencil and paper to design some personalized symbols. You can create a symbol for anything – a car, a plane, a skateboard, a pizza, a mobile phone, your mum, whatever you like. However, make sure the symbols are simple, so you can copy the shapes into clay.

Next, it's time to make a clay tablet. Take a fist-sized lump of clay and roll it out, using a rolling pin, into a square shape - about 1 cm thick. This will be your tablet.

Use the sharp stick (the stylus) to make your symbols in the clay tablet. The best thing about your own Sumerian tablet is that you don't need an attacking army to bake it - just bake it in your oven, following the instructions on the pack of modelling clay.

When your clay is baked, carefully remove it from the oven and leave to cool. Maybe a kid in 2080 will find it and use their TT handset to come back to visit you to ask what the symbols mean.

# HOW TO ...

# SURVIVE THE BLACK DEATH

Splat – you've landed in a lumpy substance that smells suspiciously like horse poo, in a filthy street in the middle of Florence, Italy.

The first thing you notice is the smell. In the 21st century, Florence is famed for magnificent art and architecture, but there isn't much evidence of that now. There's just a foul stench and a sense of impending doom. You've arrived when the city is in the grip of the 'Black Death', a deadly disease that will go on to kill around a third of all the people in Europe.

You have two options – hit the EJECT button and get out of here (it really does smell awful), or stick around to see what's going on.

## CAUTION

- The Black Death, otherwise known as the plague, is highly infectious, and can cause a painful death.

- Avoid anyone who looks sick. They may be coughing up blood that contains plague bacteria.

- Avoid rats or anywhere they might be hiding. Rats don't cause the disease, but the fleas that live on the rats do.

- Don't worry if people don't want to speak to you. Everyone is so scared – some parents have even abandoned their sick children to avoid being infected themselves.

# RUNNING SCARED

At the side of the road you see a man running along with his face covered. When you go over to speak to him he looks very afraid. However, once you have assured him that you are not infected in any way, he lets you accompany him to his house. His name is Giovanni. He apologizes for his rudeness, but explains that so many people have died from the disease everyone is now terrified. People are too scared to look after their loved ones when they are sick, or even bury them when they die.

So far nobody has found a way to stop the disease. Some people have barricaded themselves in their homes. They believe the plague is a curse from God and that by living well and praying they will escape. Other people have left the city altogether in the hope that they can outrun the disease. A few people seem to have gone mad, trying to have as much fun as possible. They drink and eat as much as they like, and steal from people's abandoned homes. They believe these are going to be their last days, so they are going to try and enjoy them as much as they can.

## MEDIEVAL MEDICINE

Giovanni has seen many people die from the disease and hasn't yet seen a treatment that has worked. Here are some of the crazy cures people have tried:

- Bloodletting. This involves cutting the body and letting the infected blood run out. This does not work and will only make the patient weaker and more likely to die.

- Cutting open the swellings caused by the disease and putting dried toads on them to draw out the poison. This would probably only result in the wounds becoming infected.

- Holding a garland of strongly scented flowers and herbs. This might block out the smell of rotting corpses, but it won't stop people from being infected. They are infected, not by the foul smell, but by the bites of infected fleas. A bunch of flowers isn't going to ward off fleas.

Giovanni stops at a door and knocks. It opens slightly and someone inside asks if he is alone. He says no and explains that you look perfectly healthy and are a traveller from a neighbouring town. There is a commotion inside and a lot of shouting. Your friend apologizes to you, but then pushes himself through the door and slams it in your face.

You look down the street and it looks completely empty. Time to go, there's nothing left for you to do here – EJECT.

## SICKLY SYMPTOMS WARNING

Phew! You're back in the present. Your TT handset is equipped with an ImmunoShield (see page 9), which protects you from catching the diseases of the past and stops you giving modern coughs and colds to the people you meet. However, in the rare event of a malfunction, look out for the following symptoms over the next few weeks:

An itchy, black, pus-filled spot. This is an infected flea-bite and may mean you are infected with the most common type of plague – bubonic plague. This can occur up to a week after having been bitten.

Swellings in your armpit or groin. These are called 'buboes' and can grow to be the size of an apple. Buboes are a sure sign that you have been infected by bubonic plague. The swellings are in fact your lymph nodes – organs in your body that work to fight against disease.

An unusual rash without buboes. This could be a sign of septicaemic plague. This is where the body is completely overwhelmed with plague bacteria and is always fatal.

Coughing up blood and a high temperature. Take care because you may have caught an even more fast-acting form of the disease, pneumonic plague. This where the plague bacteria has been transmitted in the coughed-up blood of other people and is now in your lungs.

If you feel at all unwell, seek medical attention. Modern antibiotics have proved very effective in treating the disease.

100 CE

## HOW TO ...

# ROAST A RODENT WITH A ROMAN

You have landed on a long dusty road in northern Italy. Behind you, you hear the loud crunch, crunch, crunch of marching soldiers coming towards you. Eek! It sounds like the whole Roman army is at your back. As you turn around the crunching comes to an abrupt halt. Mistaking you for one of the soldiers in his 'century', or unit of 80 men, the 'centurion', or leader of the century, tells you to get in line with the rest of the soldiers.

## A LUCKY ESCAPE

You get in line next to a soldier called Curtius Balbas. He tells you that you are very lucky to get off so lightly. Punishments in the Roman legions are very harsh. Soldiers who misbehave are flogged, and if the centurion had suspected you of making a run for it, every tenth man in the whole century could have been killed. This is called *decimatio* and the centurions use this as a warning to anyone wanting to flee from battle. Curtius says he has seen this happen before and that it is terrifying waiting to find out if it is going to be you for the chop.

# LIFE IN THE LEGIONS

Today the soldiers are on a training march. They do this three to four times a month and travel at speeds of up to 8 kilometres an hour and cover up to 30 kilometres in just five hours wearing full armour. In addition they have to carry all the things they will need to set up camp. Curtius says that training is hard going, but that it is much better than fighting or building long straight roads like the one you are walking on now. Curtius has fought in 15 campaigns since he was called to serve when he was just 17 years old.

# A GOOD MEAL

By the time you stop to make camp for the night, you are very tired. You are so hungry you could eat a horse, but Curtius has something much smaller in mind. He suggests feasting on a highly prized Roman delicacy – roasted dormouse. Dormice would usually be served at elegant banquets, but luckily for you he keeps a jar with live dormice in and feeds them up for the pot. Not wanting to sound chicken, you accept his offer and watch how he prepares his Roman rodent recipe.

## DELICIOUS DORMOUSE DELIGHT

In the present, the dormouse is a protected species, and most people don't want to eat them anyway. Curtius uses real dormice for his recipe but he says you could use chicken thighs instead.

### YOU WILL NEED:

- Four skinless, boneless chicken thighs • 100g minced pork
- 1 tbsp chopped nuts • 1 tbsp chicken stock
- 1 tbsp chopped laser (a herb found in North Africa) or sage
- salt and pepper

1. Pre-heat the oven to gas mark 6 / 200 °C / 400 °F.

2. Add the minced pork, nuts, laser (or sage), salt and pepper to a bowl and mix together thoroughly. Stir in the chicken stock.

3. Flatten out your chicken thighs and lay them so that the insides face upwards.

4. Using a tablespoon, place a dollop of the pork mixture into the middle of each thigh and then close them up.

5. Place your chicken thighs on a clay tile (or in a casserole dish) join side down and roast in the oven for 35 minutes.

6. After 35 minutes, remove your roasted Roman treats from the oven using oven gloves and leave to cool for five minutes, then serve.

**SERVING TIP:** For a sweeter treat, drizzle the roast thighs with honey and sprinkle with poppy seeds. Yummy!

1275 CE

# FOLLOW THE OLD SILK ROAD

Ouch, you've landed right between two humps on a camel's back and it hurts! It's hard to say who is more surprised, you or the camel. But there's no time to think about that, because the camel is already moving. You're off along the Old Silk Road, the ancient trading route between China and Europe.

It's not like any road you know – more like a dusty track – and you're travelling with a 'caravan', or group of merchants, and their camels. They are taking silk, tea, porcelain and other goods to trade with European merchants at trading posts and bazaars along the route. In exchange they will buy European goods such as gold, wool and wine and take them back to China.

## BANDITS

Be warned. The Old Silk Road goes through entire deserts and some of the highest mountain ranges in the world, and it's tough and dangerous to travel. You're travelling through bandit country, so watch out for ambushes. Likely places are narrow passes, dense undergrowth, and behind hilltops and large boulders. To make it harder for bandits, you can:

- Vary the speed at which you travel.

- Stop regularly, and check the route ahead and behind you.

- Keep an eye out for glints of light – it may be sunlight reflecting off something metal belonging to a crouching bandit.

- Make sure the members of your caravan are spaced out. You should aim to be close enough to help each other out, but far enough apart so that bandits can't completely surround you.

# SANDSTORMS

You're in sandstorm country, too. Strong winds blowing over loose sand or soil create enormous dust clouds that move at speeds of up to 160 kilometres per hour. If you spot one, here's what to do:

- Move to higher ground if you can.

- Cover your nose and mouth with a wet cloth.

- Try to take shelter. Look for a large rock to protect you from the worst of the sand. Alternatively, use your new friend, your camel. Make it sit down, and squeeze down next to it, on the side sheltered from the wind. Your camel will be alright. It has good protection against sandstorms. It can close its nostrils, and it has bushy eyebrows and long eyelashes to keep sand out of its eyes.

- Wrap yourself in anything you can to shield yourself. The strong winds may have scooped up heavy objects and you could be hit.

- Once the storm is with you, stay put until it's over – visibility can be reduced to zero within seconds.

## DIZZY HEIGHTS

When you reach the mountains, you'll be travelling along steep, narrow tracks with terrifying drops into ravines hundreds of metres below. If you are panicking, don't fight it. Accept that you're scared stiff. Slow down your breathing. Keep right behind the trader in front of you and follow in his camel's footsteps exactly. Look out for loose ground that could trip you up. Don't look too far ahead. Concentrate on here and now and stop worrying about that even steeper bit you can see ahead.

HOW TO ...

# GO WILD IN THE WEST

Aaaaargh! You've just landed in the middle of a river. It's icy cold. Your teeth are too frozen to even chatter. The river is wide and fast-flowing, and though it is quite shallow, the current is almost strong enough to whisk you off your feet. You grab hold of the nearest thing — an ox.

The ox is not alone. It's part of a team pulling a wagon across the river. There are more wagons up ahead, and still more behind you. In fact, there are wagons as far as your eyes can see in both directions. You have arrived in the middle of a vast train of wagons heading westward. They are filled with people who have decided to leave the towns and cities in eastern America and travel to the West in search of a new and better life. This is the West they call the Wild West!

## MAKING CAMP

Your TT handset may have state-of-the-art waterproofing, but you don't. You are drenched by the time you wade to the far bank. Luckily the wagon master who is leading the train decides this is a good spot to make camp for the night.

Soon all the wagons are arranged in a great big circle. Campfires are lit and big pots of food are cooking. You sit around the fire with your fellow travellers, singing songs and chatting under the stars. This most definitely beats your average caravanning holiday!

## IT'S TOUGH OUT WEST

Don't be fooled by the campfire songs – the people singing are pioneers, and they are tough, because life in the West is tough.

- They start their day early, lighting fires and getting breakfast on the go before dawn.

- People have to walk most of the day. The oxen are already pulling heavy loads, and the terrain is bumpy. Riding in the wagons is no fun either. You would be shaken like a rag doll, and all the pots and pans banging together make a clanking racket.

- Despite being on the trail for ten or more hours, most wagon trains can only travel about 19 kilometres a day. If it's rainy and muddy, they manage a lot less.

- The children have lots of chores – such as collecting wood, helping cook, fetching water from the river and milking cows.

# DANGERS ON THE TRAIL

Heading west can be a dangerous journey. Keep a lookout for some of the potential perils ahead.

- The trail itself is full of danger. Some of the trail is through high mountain passes and across rivers far wider, deeper and wilder than the one you just crossed.

- The Wild West is full of wildlife. There are rattlesnakes around, whose bite could kill you. Wild dogs called coyotes and other savage animals roam in the night looking for a meal.

- The sun is very hot and the ground is very dry. Grass fires can flare up at any time and can engulf slow-moving wagons.

- The prairies are very open and exposed. During storms, a lightning strike can set a wagon on fire in seconds.

- The pioneers are carrying everything they own, so these slow-moving caravans are easy targets for bandits. Bandits and outlaws are a constant threat, and they are what make the West so wild.

# FOLLOWING THE TRAIL

After a night sleeping by the campfire, you wake for another day on the trail. You decide to catch up to the wagon master at the head of the train. He gives the order for the wagons to move on. As you go along he shows you some of the signs a wagon train in front has left behind. At first they just look like piles of pebbles, but as you look more closely he explains that these piles of pebbles show you which way to go and give warnings of any dangers that lie ahead. He asks you to help him by setting signs along the trail for the pioneers trailing behind to follow. He tells you some of the different signs he uses.

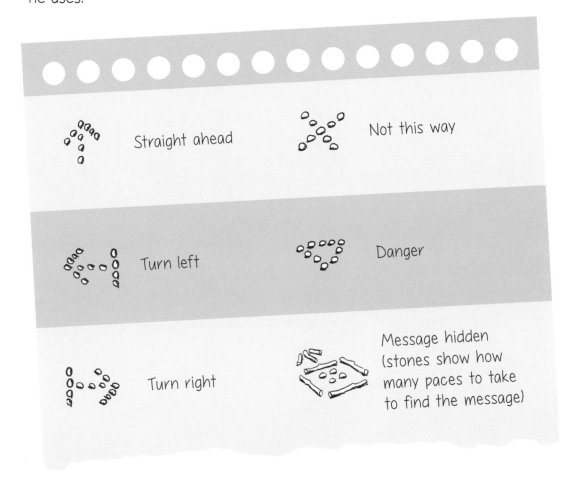

Straight ahead

Not this way

Turn left

Danger

Turn right

Message hidden (stones show how many paces to take to find the message)

**1783 CE**

# HOW TO ...

# FLY IN A HOT-AIR BALLOON

The sound of roaring hot-air burners fills your ears and you find yourself in the basket of a hot-air balloon soaring 1,000 metres above the ground. You are not in just any balloon, you are taking part in the first ever manned balloon flight.

There are two other people on board, a science teacher and an adventurer. After their initial shock on seeing you appear beside them, they tell you that the balloon was launched from the gardens of a huge house, just outside Paris. It is now soaring over the city, and has travelled about 9 kilometres, which is impressive when you consider no one has travelled through the air like this before. Below, people are dotted about like ants, cheering and waving. You wave back, enjoying your celebrity moment.

The huge balloon measures 23 metres tall and 14 metres across, with a fancy sky-blue-and-gold design all over it. It is made of a material called taffeta, which has been covered with a fireproofing varnish. Unfortunately, the fireproofing isn't really working. You can smell burning. The balloon is starting to look a bit scorched. One of the men whips off his coat and beats the flames licking up at the taffeta balloon. It is time to land.

## BALLOONING BROTHERS

You touch down between two windmills, and just in time – your TT handset is beginning to melt around the edges. Two brothers, Joseph and Étienne Montgolfier, are introduced to you. They are the brains behind this flight. Étienne has the business brain and Joseph is a mad inventor. Joseph tells you the idea of building the balloon you have just been travelling in came to him when he noticed how clothes drying over a fire billowed upwards. After five years of experimenting, voilà, he built this big balloon.

Joseph admits that you and your two companions aren't the first living creatures to make a balloon flight. That honour went to a sheep, a duck and a rooster, who were sent on an earlier flight, but no one really knows what they thought of the experience.

Time to go. You sneak off behind a tree to activate the EJECT button on your singed TT handset – just imagine how much Joseph Montgolfier would like to get his hands on a machine that flies you through time as well as space ...

**12,000 BCE**

# MAKE A FLINT AXE

Suddenly you hear the sounds of two stones being struck together behind you. You spin around and see a man sitting on the ground. He is chipping away at a large hunk of rock with a smaller rock.

He is making an axe, but when it is finished, it doesn't look like any axe you've seen before. It doesn't even have a handle. He sees you are puzzled and walks towards a small sapling. Holding the axe blade side out in the palm of his hand, he hits the sapling at the base. It comes down in one stroke. He picks it up and then uses the edge of the blade to scrape off some bark at the base. He pulls on the bark and it comes off in one long strip which he says they can use for string or for weaving baskets.

He hands you a chunk of rock which he says is flint and tells you to have a go.

## STONE AGE STEP-BY-STEP

### YOU WILL NEED:

• a large piece of flint • protective glasses • a few pebbles of different shapes and sizes • a piece of bone or hard wood • a thick leather cloth or a doubled-up towel

**1** First, select the piece of flint you will be shaping. If possible, get a piece that is already a flattish round or oval shape. Avoid flint with white veins or bits of crystal in the rock – it is not good for shaping. Also, if you tap the flint and it makes a muffled sound, this means there is a fault inside which will make it weak and difficult to 'knap', or shape into a stone tool.

**2** Rest your piece of flint on a thick leather cloth (or towel) on your left knee and steady it with your left hand if you are right-handed (the other way if you are left-handed).

**3** Use one of your pebbles to strike the longest side of the flint. Use blows to one side rather than hitting it in the middle. This will make sure you remove some long shards of flint from the edge of the rock, making it more pointed.

**4** As you knap, don't throw away the flakes you chip off. They can be made into arrowheads and small tools for scraping the flesh away from an animal skin. Be careful, they are very sharp.

**5** Once you have shaped your big piece of flint so that it looks narrower on one side than the other (this is the chopping side of the axe), you are ready to start making a sharp edge.

**6** With a smaller pebble, continue flaking off long pieces of flint in the same way as you did before – but this time, use less force, and be especially careful to knap along the long 'face' of the axe.

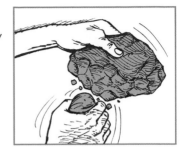

As the edge of the axe gets thinner, you'll need to use your pieces of bone or wood instead of the pebble to avoid breaking off too much flint in one go.

**7** Place the axe on a hard surface, and with the chopping side closest to the surface, grind the pointed end of your piece of wood in a twisting motion against the very edge of the axe. This will allow you to take off tiny pieces of flint until your axe is the perfect shape.

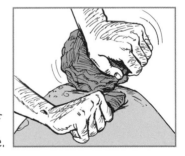

## WARNING

Shards of flint can be as sharp as kitchen knives. Wear protective glasses and be sure to cover your lap. Be very careful when getting rid of shards of flint. Wrap them in several sheets of newspaper and throw them in the bin.

Never knap flint indoors, as rock dust can be very bad for your lungs.

800 CE

# BEAT THE MAYA AT BALL

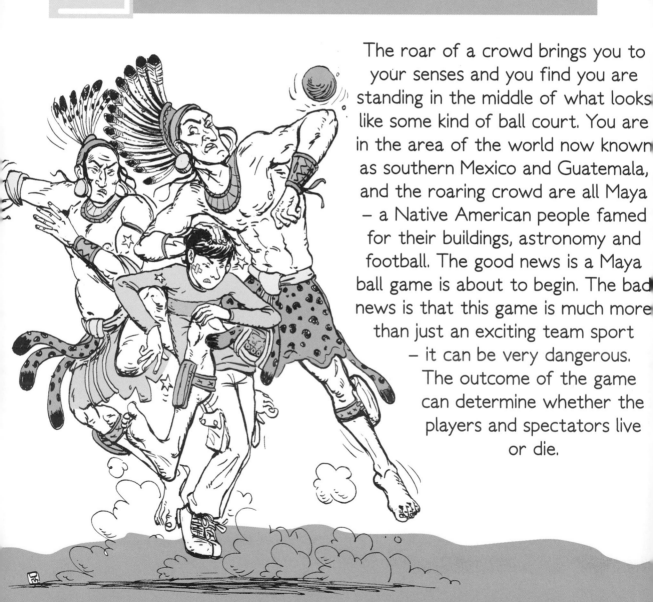

The roar of a crowd brings you to your senses and you find you are standing in the middle of what looks like some kind of ball court. You are in the area of the world now known as southern Mexico and Guatemala, and the roaring crowd are all Maya – a Native American people famed for their buildings, astronomy and football. The good news is a Maya ball game is about to begin. The bad news is that this game is much more than just an exciting team sport – it can be very dangerous. The outcome of the game can determine whether the players and spectators live or die.

## LET'S PLAY BALL

The ball court you are standing in is shaped like a capital letter 'I', with high sides decorated with elaborate carvings. The high sides help to keep the ball in play.

For the game itself, you are going to need to strip off and put on some gear to protect you from injury. The ball is made of solid rubber. It can weigh as much as 4 kilograms and is hard enough to break your bones. So make sure you strap on some padded shin, knee and forearm protectors made from animal skin. Think yourself lucky, though – the ball was sometimes made from a human skull wrapped in strips of rubber to make it bounce nicely.

Pop on your feathered headdress and you are ready to play ball. You look a-Maya-zing – as do the other members of your team, who enter the court wearing their finest animal skins, feather headdresses and jewellery.

## MAYA RULES

Now this is the tricky part: historians aren't sure exactly how this game was played. So you are going to have to keep your wits about you. What previous time travellers do know, however, is that you should try really hard to help your team win, because the losers are often sacrificed to the gods.

Take a look at the end of the court. You will notice that there is a stone ring, just large enough for the ball to fit through. It is probably a wise move to aim for that. Make sure that you are whacking the ball in the right direction – own goals aren't good no matter which century you are in.

# THE TIMELINE

The LEAP button on your TT handset carries you back in time at random. However, if you wanted to travel back following the historical order in which the events in this book happened, this timeline shows you the route you would travel. It starts from the present day and ends up back in the time of the dinosaurs.

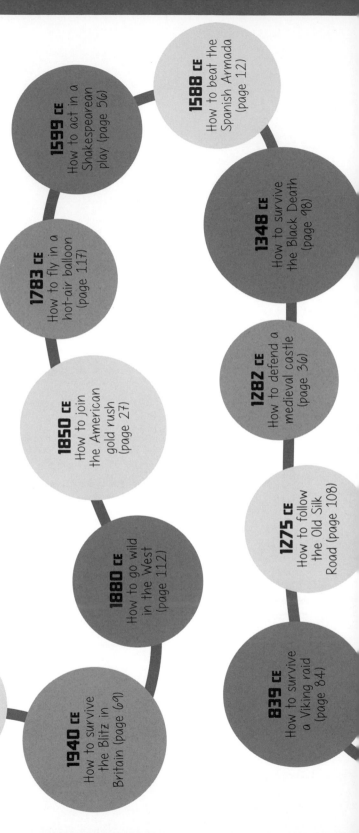

**NOW**

**1969 CE**
How to walk on the Moon (page 60)

**1940 CE**
How to survive the Blitz in Britain (page 69)

**1880 CE**
How to go wild in the West (page 112)

**1850 CE**
How to join the American gold rush (page 27)

**1783 CE**
How to fly in a hot-air balloon (page 117)

**1599 CE**
How to act in a Shakespearean play (page 56)

**1588 CE**
How to beat the Spanish Armada (page 12)

**1348 CE**
How to survive the Black Death (page 98)

**1282 CE**
How to defend a medieval castle (page 36)

**1275 CE**
How to follow the Old Silk Road (page 108)

**839 CE**
How to survive a Viking raid (page 84)

This is what the symbols on page 95 mean.

Head

Walk

Water

**70 Million BCE**
How to tackle a
T. Rex (page 48)

**40,000 BCE**
How to hunt
a mammoth
(page 20)

**17,000 BCE**
How to paint a
cave (page 32)

**12,000 BCE**
How to make
a flint axe
(page 120)

**3100 BCE**
How to invent
writing with
the Sumerians
(page 94)

**2500 BCE**
How to make
papyrus in
ancient Egypt
(page 24)

**1550 BCE**
How to make
an Egyptian
mummy
(page 79)

**1500 BCE**
How to leap
a Minoan bull
(page 74)

**1450 BCE**
How to write
in hieroglyphs
(page 88)

**700 BCE**
How to
make silk in
ancient China
(page 16)

**480 BCE**
How to compete
at the ancient
Olympics
(page 43)

**100 CE**
How to roast
a rodent with
a Roman
(page 104)

**108 CE**
How to graduate
from gladiator
school (page 64)

**800 CE**
How to beat the
Maya at ball
(page 124)

**832 CE**
How to build a
Viking longship
(page 52)

# CONGRATULATIONS

## This is to certify that

......................................

## is now a

**BUSTER KNOW-HOW EXPERT**